STRUCTURAL LYRICISM

STRUCTURAL LYRICISM
Poetry Without Metaphor
by J. A. Gucci

Standard Edition

ISBN: 978-1-972788-17-2

Printed in the United States of America

For information about the instructor edition of this work, contact: www.jagucci.com

This book is a work of art. The poems are composed as systems of transformation. Any interpretation arises from the reader's engagement with the structure.

Contents

Preface 7

Opus I 11
Opus II 12
Opus III 13
Opus IV 14
Opus V 15
Opus VI 16
Opus VII 17
Opus VIII 18
Opus IX 19
Opus X 20

Opus XI 21
Opus XII 22
Opus XIII 23
Opus XIV 24
Opus XV 25
Opus XVI 26
Opus XVII 27
Opus XVIII 28
Opus XIX 29
Opus XX 30

Opus XXI 31
Opus XXII 32
Opus XXIII 33
Opus XXIV 34
Opus XXV 35
Opus XXVI 36
Opus XXVII 37

Opus XXVIII 38
Opus XXIX 39
Opus XXX 40

Opus XXXI 41
Opus XXXII 42
Opus XXXIII 43
Opus XXXIV 44
Opus XXXV 45
Opus XXXVI 46
Opus XXXVII 47
Opus XXXVIII 48
Opus XXXIX 49
Opus XL 50

Afterword 51
Author's Note 52
Colophon 53

Preface

These poems are composed as systems.

Each presents a transformation. A condition holds,
is altered, and does not return unchanged. The
movement is structural. It is not explained.

The poems do not begin with theme or narrative.
They are built from observable conditions and the
changes those conditions undergo. What appears is
what occurs.

Meaning is not assigned in advance. It arises
through arrangement.

The sequence is intentional. Variation in density,
pacing, and compression shapes the reading
experience. Some transformations are immediate.
Others are delayed or absent.

No additional framework is required. The poems
stand on their own.

On Absolute Composition

These poems are constructed within a compositional framework developed in Absolute Composition: Structure, Threshold, and Compression in Poetry.

In that framework, a poem is organized as a system. A condition holds, crosses a threshold, and becomes another condition. Meaning does not precede this movement. It arises from arrangement.

No additional explanation is required here.

The poems present what occurs. Structure carries the experience.

The arrangement is sufficient.

"The arrangement is sufficient."

Opus I

I sit by the waning fire
on top of a snowy hill,
shoulder to shoulder—
with you.

Gaze at a faint
flickering star—
with you.

Embers—
plumes of white,
ash—

constellation.

Opus II

Barefoot on damp soil,
we walk—
apricot sky.

Propped on a moonlit sand bar,
still lake—
knee to knee,
hand in hand,

I whisper—
shimmering moon.

Opus III

My blood—
a gift,
pulsing in her veins,
breath—
thirst.

Because I love you
inexorably—

a whim.

Opus IV

Glance—
gaze—
across the crowded hall—
at me.

Her listless eyes—
perusing,
drifting,

falter—
I flatten a napkin
crumpled.

Opus V

Cradled in a dry creek bed
sheltered by a rock slab,
ensconced—
you and I.

Rumbles—
damp air—
a flock hovers
over a scree slope.

Splayed—
you and I,
over black sands—
sheltered by a warm
vibrating hill.

Opus VI

Your smiling face
dangling on a wire—
dripping and drying.

I kiss your lips,
gaze—
into your eyes—

Nora.

Opus VII

Strolling in the square—
foggy,
at dusk—
we laugh till dawn.

Zenith—
sharp shadows
under feet,
elongating—

melded.

Opus VIII

Stands of gold
draped over skin,
olive—
chestnut eyes,
pink puckered
lips.

Tears at dawn,
dusk—
slumped in a settee,
still
swaying.

Who are you?

Opus IX

I wander through the field—
kick up a stone,
chase a whirling pod
downstream.

I fold her woolen sweater,
socks,
starch a collar—
sew a button.

Stacked—
pile of cotton,
teetering—

footprints in the snow.

Opus X

Your words
linger,
loom—

I toss,
turn—

drop to the floor—
cracked frame.

Opus XI

Splayed in a settee
still,
swaying—
cucumbers in water
over ice.

I reach for the phone
again,
her voice—
polite,
mechanical again.

Slumped in a sette—
still,
swaying—
cucumbers in water.

Opus XII

Slip-stitched—
ivory pearls,
a peal,
shiny stockings.

Perfect black
body—

guffaw.

Opus XIII

Nude in a glade—
a thicket of foxgloves,
we sing,
dance—
draws circles in silt,
dry—

light—
plumes of smoke,
ash—

hunkered in a cave—
sweaty,
sooty skin.

Opus XIV

Slumped in a white
wicker chair—
olive pillow,

swaying on a glider,
quilted blanket—

illuminated by the oil lamp
resting on the ledge.

Breeze—
charred cotton air—
dusk,

we settle
asleep—

twitch.

Opus XV

She waves her hand,
throws a stone,
bellows—
at me.

But I gaze at the snow
blowing across the trail,
nip of brandy—
a long, slow drag;
and wait—

hiss.

Opus XVI

Downstroke—
blonde strands
over shoulders
supple.

Upstroke—
blue,
chestnut dripping—

seeping into white
linen—

blotch.

Opus XVII

I whisper in a corner—
tiled,
arched—
to her.

Before a second,
she turns—

secret.

Opus XVIII

Table set for two—
ceramic cups,
saucers

made from broken vases—
steaming,

tepid.

Opus XIX

Center floor—
she and I,
pressed together—
poised.

Down bow—
a step forward,
detache—
back,
tremolo—

pirouette.

Opus XX

Old hollow body—
sheep guts,
taut around a headstock.

Plucked—
she sings to me!

Desafinado.

Opus XXI

Lips puckered—
cemented,

your face,
rosy glow—
quivers.

Lustrous black
fur,
yellow eyes—

vault—
splayed on her lap—

cat kiss.

Opus XXII

Flacon—
empty on the plinth—

I reach for the phone—

sweet amber air.

Opus XXIII

She spins—
slowly,
holding a moment
midair.

"How do I look?"

Poached meringue—
Île Flottante… à la Luna—

sullen.

Opus XIV

Throb—
wet,
undulating flytrap—

sealed,
airtight—

mucilage.

Opus XXV

I listen—
piddling bellows,
with an ear—

stifle a yawn—
smile,

kiss good night.

Opus XXVI

Stern,
bow—

drifting—
glints and glitter,

I rise—
she trims the gunwale,

bow—
stern.

Opus XXVII

My sooty hands,
greasy denim.

Silk blouse,
hair bun.

Clean—
linen trousers,

strands of blonde
draped over her shoulder.

Cigarettes and scotch—
neat,

an orgasm on the rocks—
cherry.

Opus XXVIII

Lipstick lapels—
numbers on a napkin—
crumpled,
late suppers.

Dust—
alight on the vanity,

her ring—
tucked in the drawer.

Opus **XXIX**

Gourmand—
tuxedo shirt,

tossed in the hamper—

musky sun dress.

Opus XXX

Hoop—
glistening gold
under mat.

Silver clinking,
throat clear—

I swallow—
thrumming treadmill.

Opus XXXI

Green earring—
chalky,
dangling on a hook,

slammed—
shuddering door—

splinters.

Opus XXXII

Trotting
side by side
around the palisades,
laughing—

riveted:
horn toot,
an air kiss—

sob—
soggy tank.

Opus XXXIII

Draped over shoulders
blonde and twirled

long and thick
brown—curled

ochre umber
almond eyes

throb—
beneath her skin,
my chest—

rapid—
shallow breaths,
flushed—

dizzying,
stuttering—

I look—
away.

Opus XXXIV

Speak to me no more—
your words cut
flesh.

I hear your voice—
static radio,

listen to the shell hum—
tidal wave.

Opus XXXV

Awake with a kiss—
sun dried apricots
drenched with honey,
ristretto—

I sneeze—
swollen throat—
damp
grey skin—

repose.

Opus XXXVI

Clean burning fire,
pumpkin soup air,
I knead her shoulders—
butter her buns.

And I—
repose on frozen planks,
splintered wood—

gutted.

Opus XXXVII

She smiles,
steps behind satin glass—

soap and cedar,
steam—

dappled light—
crescent.

Opus XXXVIII

Enfolded on satin sheets—

glissando—
trill—

cadence.

Opus XXXIX

Bordeaux on my placket—

she blots,
wipes,

scrubs,
scrapes—

a sprig of thyme—
dipped in holy water.

Opus XL

I love you

but,

not enough.

Afterword

These poems were composed through attention to change.

Each begins from a condition that can be observed. What follows is not explanation but arrangement. A surface alters. A boundary is crossed, delayed, or withheld. What remains is presented without commentary.

Across the sequence, patterns recur. Some transformations are immediate. Others disperse. In certain cases, the crossing is no longer visible, and only its effect persists. The variation is structural.

No single reading is required. The poems do not direct interpretation. They present conditions and their alteration. The reader encounters the result.

The work proceeds by accumulation. Each piece stands on its own, but the sequence intensifies through repetition and difference. Density increases, then loosens. Certain movements return in altered form.

Nothing has been added to clarify what the structure already carries. Nothing has been removed that would compromise the transformation.

What holds remains.

Author's Note

J. A. Gucci writes poetry organized around
systems, thresholds, and compression. The work
focuses on transformation across observable
conditions without reliance on narrative program
or embedded metaphor.

The poems in this book were composed over time
through sustained attention to structure. They are
presented here without additional framing.

An instructor edition of this work presents the
structural frameworks underlying these poems.

Colophon

This book was set in Palatino.

Designed and composed by the author.

Printed in the United States of America.

Standard Edition.